Love
That Hurts . . .
Is the Love That
Heals!

Love
That Hurts . . .
Is the Love That Heals!

Om Sai Ram !!

Daisy Raj Singh

PARTRIDGE

Copyright © 2016 by Daisy Raj Singh.

ISBN:	Hardcover	978-1-4828-8601-6
	Softcover	978-1-4828-8600-9
	eBook	978-1-4828-8599-6

Print information available on the last page.

To order additional copies of this book, contact
Partridge India
000 800 10062 62
orders.india@partridgepublishing.com

www.partridgepublishing.com/india

CONTENTS

ACKNOWLEDGEMENTS

This book is dedidated to all the people who have filled my life with love and an undying support.

To
Mom & Dad

Dad: My Hero...The Late Commandant Lakhwant Singh,
I know you are watching us from above.

Hope this makes you proud!

He always believed that we were here to achieve. He taught us to live with Honesty, Determination and gave us the strength to voice our opinions without fear.

Mom: The most beautiful and stylish lady with an Iron will. She has maintained her poise &dignity in the most trying situations and has taught us to face life.

My 2 sisters, Vipen di &Honey: for bearing with my eccentricities, like the changing of my nail paint every 2 minutes....till I was satisfied.

My brother Sunny: Yes, I am baised about you...for you are the most darling brother a sister can dream of.
Though a tough task master, you have always pushed me to my limits only to bring out the best in me.

My sister in law, Kanwal: Beautiful, thanks for always believing in me & for all the love and pampering.

My Son: Angad ....You breathed life into me....Thanks son for always being a part of my social work even at the tender age of 4yrs, you gave your services to the needy...with those tiny hands.

My beautiful neices Tutu &Sannah: Thanks for taking after me. That does make me proud.

My brother in law: Rj for being the person he is.

My husband: For always challenging my strengths, and see I won!

Now all those who I was blessed with,
My extended family:

Mrs Surubhi Raha: My friend, Philosopher &guide.

Kamlesh: Your spiritual support gave me the strength when I thought I had none.

Rangta: The most honest opinions I got from, thank you for showing me parts of me I never thought existed.

Chubba: A son from another mother, your principles I adore, my most trusted one.
Nini: My doll.

Saket: Love to hear you call me Ma.

Dr Dasgupta: The most well read man to have come across and my father figure.

Riya, Piya, Rohit, Riju, Ahmad,

...who taught me the naunces of the computer and the leaders of the mad brigade Rydakians!

Fateh Bajwa: Thanks for listening to all my bickering for hours and leaving me with a surprise question each time!

Richard &Tanu: for refuelling my soul.

My school friends, Anil, Rajat, Geet, Abhishek, Sundari, Heena and all my KV Lamphel friends, 93 batch, as eccentric as me...We rock guys!

Bobby: a friend who doesnt give up on my dreams even when I am tired.

All my AR brats...for we have grown together and the love has increased manifold over the years. Thanks for pampering me spoilt.

&

Nomi: My soul sister!Thanks for going through the torture of listening to my Poems "n" number of times...even when you are sleepy and I am totally excited at 1 O'clock at night.
Without you my friend I would not have been here today. My Italian beauty....you are my most precious gift from God!

This is where I found "ME"!!!

1. SOULMATE

I was lost in the deep dark woods,
Shadows of darkness on my soul,
Mist in the eyes,
Bleeding was the bruised innocence,
A heart shattered as pieces from a broken pane....

Then came a voice...from the unknown,
So sure, so pure, so my very own,
I looked around,
Only to be filled with emotions
long lost and forgotten.

Said to me the eloping darkness,
Weakened by the heavenly persuasion,
"This is the voice of your Resonating Soul
having crossed a million miles.....
Reaching its destination.....
It is.....
YOUR SOULMATE.....!!

2. DESERT

I was walking alone,
The mirage of my dreams.
The sun shone brightly,
On my soul....parched to breathe.

I was crumbling, into specks of dust.
Sieving broken pieces was I, lost
in the desert hot sand...

Out of nowhere came a hand,
To hold mine, held me close ...so close,
To breath air into my dying soul.

Lost in those arms,
I found myself whole again,
I found myself whole again...!!

3. THE SILVER OAKS

Walking amidst the silver oaks,
     Hand in hand we walk beyond...
the shadows of darkness and being alone,
     into the abode we call home.
Where you paint the colours of love,
     Of our unison, our very own
Wrapped into each other, we go on
     Moving ahead and beyond.
As the moonlit and starry nights,
     Brought the twinkle in your eyes,
As tender as rose petals, your lips fell on mine,
     We go on, far and beyond
Into the abode we call home.
     We go on........

4. HOPE & FAITH

I walk beside you Hope &Faith,
Hold my hand with a lot of zeal,
My pain is about to heal.
Hold me closer, hold me tight,
I am about to win the fight!

As we welcome the new moon
The silver around, pierces the blinds
of fear and despair,
I walk beside you Hope & Faith.

We walked a cumbersome journey,
Hand in hand, willing to survive.
The night was dark and lasted long,
Reached have the rays of the sun,
on the morning due
I walk beside you Hope & Faith
To let the Daisy's bloom,
To let the Daisy's bloom...!!

5. SILENCE

Today my words are mute,
Resonating the echoes of a sobbing soul.
My tears hide behind the kohl,
Never to flow, into nothingness.

I may never be able to say why...
I may never be able to say how...
I lost my way ....into the oblivion.

But I do know....
One day, My Silence will have a voice of its own
Shattering the walls I build, around my soul.

And,
My world shall never be mute again
My world shall never be mute again.

6. OH! MY SELFLESS MOON

The moon steals the darkness of the night,
In all subtlety, glorifies the Love...
Of two aching souls twined together in thoughts.
The moon humbly, plays the cupid
Travelling a hundred miles each night,
To bring solace to the parched hearts
For the pain is excruciating,
To be separated....
As the moon shies away,
Into selfish mornings.

Oh! My selfless Moon,
As you come again,
You hang upside down,
By your silver tinted arms,
The soul mates finding Bliss,
Waiting for the night to dawn.

Oh! My selfless Moon,
In your subtlety,
You glorify the Love- Unknown
Oh! you glorify the Love- Unknown...!!

7. IT'S JUST A MATTER OF TIME

Oh Baby, let me wrap my aching arms around you,
Take you in and hold you tight.
As slowly you rest your head on my bosom,
Can you not hear my heartbeats, call out your name!

Oh Baby, you are mine,
It's just a matter of time.

Let me please steal you for a moment
from your world,
As in this moment, my lonesome world thrives.

Oh Baby, you are mine,
Its just a matter of time.

As I close my eyes, to feel your touch
My parched lips tenderly brushed by yours
We melt into unison.....

Oh Baby, you are mine,
Its just a matter of time.

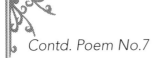

Contd. Poem No.7

Let me hold you tight,
However foolishly we might fight,
Let me hold your hand and walk you to the land of our dreams.

Oh Baby, you are mine,
Its just a matter of time....

Hold on just a little longer
The bond is even stronger
So darling, its just a matter of time

Baby, you are forever mine,
When you are for ever.....mine!!

8. EXPRESSIONS OF A BLEEDING HEART

Let me express, Oh! My Love,
The days are numbered,
The Love is eternal & the Love is pure,
True to its very core.

Let me express, Oh! My Love, let me.....

The day we first met,
Your lil'flirtations stole my heart,
The twinkle in your eyes lit my soul.

I blushed, and my whole being stirred,
As the milestone of my life, touched its mid -term score,
I was dancing on my toes, as a ballerina 15yrs old.

The season changed,
The autumn of yesteryears,
Blossomed into the spring long on hold.

Baby, so the yearning grew and
grew the pain,
Reigning a heart so deeply in love,
brought the winters back.

Contd. Poem No.8.

Let me express, Oh! My Love....the days are numbered.

We were soulmates, I was told
We understood without saying a word,
The songs of our soul.

In that deep voice when you called my name,
The tenderness touched me,
like the warmth of a mother's womb.

Today I am lost and I am cold,
I have to chain the feelings and let go.....
In all humbleness, Baby
My love was a gift to Thee, so nurtured for ages
&
not just phases, My love.

I'll heal or I'll bleed
The wounds are too deep,
But to me they too are a gift of love,
By the shadows of my soul,
So very precious, so very my own.

I would nurture I, would still care
Never will I need to share
Never will I need to share.

9. THE PRINCESS

The eyes behold the story of a Princess,
Of trial and triumphs.
She hides behind a facade ....from the world
she calls her own,
For, she is the Princess!

Behind the silks of her veil,
She silently weeps,
Building walls of gold around her heart and soul,
For, she is the Princess!

Each tear is the story of strength,
Each battle so well fought,
She walks with grit, the gait of a lioness.
Feet firmly on the ground,
She reaches out for the moon.
For, she is the Princess!

Deep inside she nurtures a silent prayer, though,
For there comes a moment in life,
Where she could just let go....
And meet that one Man,
She could run to....
And call out loud....

Contd. Poem No.9

"In your arms behold....
For I have held together for so long
Oh! My Prince, Behold.....
For I have held together for so long"....!!!

10. THE BANYAN TREE

As I sit under the banyan tree,
I hear the cuckoo sing in glee,
The glory of Love,
Weaving its abode with strings,
Of promises so well kept.

As I hear the cuckoo coo,
My heart craves to be singing too,
The tales of my love, I so believed in you!

But,
Days went by and rolled in years,
Eyes have now forsaken the tears.

I still sit under the Banyan tree,
With abated breath I wait for Thee,
Thou shalt not break this heart,
With unkept promises and fake dreams.

I hear the crumbling leaves, beneath,
The harsh winters and, on the barren tree,
I still hear the cuckoo sing,
To the warmth of the promises fulfilled.

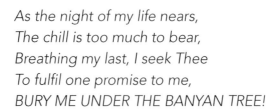

Contd. Poem No.10

As the night of my life nears,
The chill is too much to bear,
Breathing my last, I seek Thee
To fulfil one promise to me,
BURY ME UNDER THE BANYAN TREE!

For I love to hear the cuckoo sing,
Basking in the glory of love,
The love....that I could never be.

11. DADDY YOUR GAIRL AWAITS....

You promised to be back in a fortnight,
Daddy, your lil'girl sits by the window sil, waiting for you to return.

The frock you bought for my birthday,
The frills are in tatters now,
Holding on to the tiny threads of hope.

You loved it when my face glowed,
Even a pimple was chagesheeted,
Today I am all bruised & my soul bleeds.

Daddy, you held my hand and led me through,
the busiest paths of life.
Today I am lost at the crossroads.

I have waited innumerable fortnights, the last decade,
Oh! Daddy, your lil'girl is cold now,
The winters have been harsh,
Having the warmth of your arms around,
was my safest haven.
Today the vultures of time hover around.

Contd. Poem No.11.....

You are in God's Grace I am told,
To your promise I still hold....my last breath
Come home Daddy....your little girl wants to sleep
Holding you tight....never to loose my grip again!

12. MIRAGE

As I woke up from the deep slumber of an ignorant bliss,
Came the truth, tearing the soul apart,
You, were just a Mirage!

In my deep dark existence of futile hope,
You, were just a Mirage!

Your soul once resonating, the depth unknown...
To the vast desert of sadness buried deep in mine,
Alas! but, you were just a Mirage.

Foolish was I,
To have bathed my parched sou, I
In the hallucination
People called Love....

For,
You were just a Mirage!!

13. SILENCE- ODE TO MY BELOVED

When all that words create, is an empty scatter
Silence is my gift to Thee.

Thou mistook my dialogue to be mere words,
Spoken by the mortal flesh,
Alas! It was my soul sewing the tatters to yours....to be whole again.

The sobs of your maidens heart, fill the melancholic skies,
Once the murmurs had filled your heart with glee.
Never will my chatter leave the walls, I now build around me
For,
Perish in silence will I.

As death wraps its arms around my listless being
ODE to you, My Beloved....
Is this persisting Silence!!

14. THE MASK

My Pen refuses to pour, for my words were pure
Disillusioned I am, for the mask has fallen,
Farce it was,
All a fake.....Resonates the pen now!

But it aches...for behind the mask
Lies a horrid truth
that burns the innocence of the soul.

My Pen refuses to pour....
My Pen refuses to pour....anymore!!

15. LET'S HEAL TOGETHER IN LOVE

Let me sew your tatters to mine
Lets heal together in love.

When your soul bleeds, so does mine
So baby, lets heal together in love.

When your angelic heart is bruised by the devil,
Let us put together the devil to rest,
For the Lord created Thee & filled love in thine heart
So lets heal together in love.

Your words are Psalms to my being,
When the devil speaks comes the darkness,
And I have always known...Its not your own,
Lets together light a lamp & heal My Love.

Let me sew your tatters to mine
&
Lets heal together in love.....!!

16. LAST WISH

With so much passion...so much of me, I put
So meagre is left, of this....me!
There melting in the scorching heat,
Weeps the soul of me, in wait of Thee.

Pray....embrace would I the end,
With Thy arms around me,
The last breath hangs around the corpse
so shamelessly in Pride.

Kiss will my mate....to let my soul go
Kiss will my mate....to let my soul go....!!!

17. I SHALL

When the silence screams
My heart silently weeps
Nursing the dagger pierced so deep, for
It was a gift of Thee.

The days are numbered,
The lonesome soul, peeps into the oblivion
To get a glimpse of Thee,
Far away, pushed by fate.

With an ounce of life, left in me
I shall reach you someday, somehow.
For Soulmates are meant to be,
For Soulmates are meant to be.

18. HE ASKED.....

Did I promise you the moon....he asked
No....said me.

Did I promise you the stars....he rebuked.
No....said me.

Then.....?

You were the Sun,
To light up the dark...wept I
But you chose to melt me bit by bit
Till no more was left ...of me.

19. FAKE IS THE ILLUSION

Am I disillusioned by an illusion, I ask Thee
For I seek more than meets the eye.

My Faith is fuelled by my resistance
To settle for less than WE.

There may be darkness around, for all to see
But this heart is filled with Hope, so to illuminate my path to Thee.

Too deep is my belief, to be shattered
By these tiny pebbles, carelessly pelted at me.

For I shall treasure each gift.

The thorns will I pluck, bleed and nurture
The budding garden of red Rose.

The satins are not ruffled so easily
By a sudden gust of wind.

However harsh the winters be, it ends
For spring to seep in, in full galore.

Contd. Poem No.19

There will be a moment so "Perfect",
Sprawled around lit candles, laced with lavender,
Music filling the sky of Thy laughter.

Am I to be disillusioned then, by an illusion....!

20. THE BLEEDING PALMS

My hands feel rough today,
Yes, they do.
I crawled on them, when my feet gave away,
To the torturous terrain,
I climb each day,
To get a glimpse of Thee.

There were thorns sprawled over Thy path,
I spread my palm,
To cushion each step you took to the summit,
And so, bruised are the hands,
But, gratified is my heart.

For I bleed for my Beloved,
But Yes, so the hands feel rough.

21. SCREECHING HOLLOWS

I am at a loss of words today,
For all I fear is the screeching hollows.

To build each concrete,
I bleed through my pen.

Into the solitary confinement,
I shall adorn my listless being,
Beading into pearls, these bits of broken me.
For, Thee praises beauty.

Silently weeps this "Blue" heart,
Wish my pen fed on ink,
But it took the better of me.

And,
Still failed to deliver,
Me of my pain & to Thee....
The pleas of a dying soul.
So true, yet so blue.....!

Hence, the fear of the screeching hollows.

22. YES MY LOVE, LIFE GOES ON.....

The tresses are laden with salt and pepper,
But the dreams are yet so colourful.

Though I need spectacles, to read my horoscope,
But the eyes are yet to loose their twinkle,
For, I still love to read between your smiles.

The ears need more decibel,
But the calm in the soul is yet to reach.

So what,
If age loves to climb up the ladder,
Its yet to raise our hearts from sixteen.

Yes, you are right My Love
Life....goes on.

We may crumble to dust our worldly attire
But yes, My Love
Life goes on....
From here.... to another level.

23. MOON & THE TIDE

The moon glorifies love
Each time a tide comes home
Embracing the shore
For, I yearn this unison
Night after night
Dance will I in ecstasy
In my beloved's arms
For the moon shall bring him to me
As the tide reaches home
Embracing the shore....One more time.

24. PEACH SUNSHINE

Peach sunshine shines Thy tresses
Soft glow of love
O 'maiden Thy beauty spell bounds me
With simplicity you rule my world....!!!

25. DEAFENING SILENCE

So silent were the nights,
And,
Deafening with the whimpers of the aching souls.

Engulfed in darkness was the world & beyond,
In it's ignorance it slept,
Oblivious to the pains the night felt.

For the souls were from far beyond,
From, any distance &time on the whole.

Time, for them had to stop,
For how untiring was the night,
Bestowing upon them,
Dreams they dread to dream.

Breathing into each other the vows,
They silently rose,
From the slumber to the aisle.

No more silent was the night.

26. MY LOVE

Give me your fears,
Give me your tears,
Give me all your pain,
Give me your broken soul.

I'll give you smiles,
With you I'll walk those extra miles,
I'll sew your tatters to mine
&
Make you whole again, My Love.

When your voice starts to quiver,
Worry not, My Love!
Just whisper my name,
I'll pour music into your cracking soul,
For you do that to mine.

As you said, love is not a bed of roses,
Cry not, when the thorns pierce your soul,
I'll be there nursing your wounds,
Soon, as I am done, picking the thorns.

27. MY GIFT FROM THEE

When God said, "As you wish" in His chapter of life,
I silently had whispered a prayer for us.

Let not the hurdles slow you down,
For I will be jumping each barricade for you.

Fear not the unending nights,
In the darkness, look for the stars in my eyes,
You will see yourself there, shinning the brightest of them all.

Tomorrow is not for us to see,
I will be there beautifying
Your each today,
I promise....My Love.

For you are my gift of Thee,
For you are my gift of Thee.

28. THE GRACEFUL GREYS

The grey tresses, traces back,
A long lost story,
Of time once lived, loved & lost.

Dreams faded in time,
And so did the dark silver hue,
I shall not regret the greys,
For that was a gift from Thee.

The mirror mocks,
Of broken promises,
Picking up pieces of a shattered soul,
I bleed......
Draining my dark silk of life.

But,
My Graceful Greys,
I shall not regret Thou,
As you are my gift from Thee.

29. CLUELESS

You always left me breathless, My love
Alas! never to raise but this time
I watch helplessly, as you leave.

Clueless I pick pieces of my shattered soul,
Reminiscing with each prick,
The moments lived,
When our souls danced in unison.

My tattered soul questions my belief,
Answers I have none,
As I watch helplessly, you leave.

Lifeless eyes sob through the dark nights,
I call out your name to the skies, helpless.
May the quivering whispers reach your far etched soul,
One more time, My Love!
May the misty winds rustle your hair, one more time,
Soothing your demons, just one more time.

Pray!
May you love, just love one more time.

30. THE DURGA IN ME

I know her name and I know her pain,
I know her, aimlessly dangling her feet
in a puddle of rain.

I know her eyes have cried,
I know her heart has tried,
But what I also know is....

That she is the DURGA in me
For the day I know this,
The world is Mine....
Yes, the world is mine!!

31. I AM VULNERABLE, FOR I CHOOSE TO BE

Meet the girl in me, as pretty as can be
For I have a heart of gold, that never goes cold
However harsh the winters be.

The twinkle in my eyes, behold that winters can be...
I believe in fairy tales to be true,
For I believe in you!

You will see me smile at every mile,
Distances do not matter to me,
For my resilience is for all to see.

I wear my attitude as a crown,
Never in sorrow shall I drown,
For I am a Princess,
As tough as can be!

Nor shall I ever let you down,
For promises I keep,
And my actions speak...
To all and sundry.

Contd. Poem 31.

I know the game well before you play,
I choose to ignore,
I choose my way,
So, if I choose to walk away
Count your sin...

I am vulnerable for I want to be,
I drop my guard to let you in,
So don't be proud at your win!
For a Princess, only love can spin,
The wheels of fortune in your name.

You are worldly, I am wise
You chose what just looked nice,
And you missed a diamond for a pebble
That is where...was all the trouble!

Had you judged like a king,
All the bliss I could bring.
Alas! But you lost,
For I am the Princess, my daddy said.
I have the strength,
I have the pride,
I am happy....I am Me,
I am happy....For, I am Me.

32. THE WILLOW TREE

She sat under the willow tree,
Clutching herself so tight, for no one to see,
The tears that bled from her heart.

She was bruised all over,
Hiding wounds that time could never heal,
Under the silken hue of her beautiful gown.

In solitude and in pain,
She whispered a name,
For only hope had kept her going.

Spring it was, in full bloom
The flowers were whispering & the birds chirped,
Happiness all over the meadow spread,
He is here, He is here....!

She saw him resting, under the willow tree,
Sadness of a bruised soul, she could see,
Of stories untold
&
Battles fought
He smiled the brightest smile!

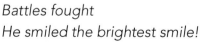

Contd. Poem 32.

Their eyes met, the silence spoke
of the thousand miles travelled.
Her soul stirred,
His laughter was a lions roar,
Filled her with pride
for soon she was to be his bride.

So lost were they in each other's arms
that time could never slow them down,
The sun shied behind the darkened skies,
The moon silently rose
splashing silver on the beautiful souls,
Uniting after ages unknown,
The stars danced in ecstasy
Such was the Bliss!

Alas! There was an evil eye,
As he healed, he chose to go,
He believed he needed her no more.
So enticed was he by the darkness,
Much to her dismay, evil had charmed her way!

She begged, pleaded him to stay,
Soulmates, they were
But......

Contd Poem.32.

His heart was clouded by the evil's charm
for he would hear no more,
Deaf was he to her heart wrenching cries,
He stabbed her in the heart,
for answers he had none.

She crumbled to dust,
Fate had so mocked her existence.....

The Willow weeps to this day,
For such could not be her fate,
The Willow weeps......to this day!!!

33. TRUTH OR DARE

I find petty minds talking loud,
To be heard and are they proud!

My, My! This world to me,
Is such a drama queen.

When the masks fall, in between,
It's truth or dare I love to ask,
Another layer, another mask, then falls…!!

34. ROWS HER BOAT AWAY

You shall be in my prayers, she said
as she rowed her boat away,
To ease him of his dilemma.

Walked on thorns she had,
Bled for years in vain
to breathe some life into his capsizing veins.

As his cheeks flushed red, with life,
He spat venom
calling her a toxic encounter.

She smiled,
Knowing her journey had come to an end.
She had cured him
flushing venom out of his being.
For, now he would live.

She could now walk with her head held high,
The love was great, and, so was her pride!

Contd. Poem 34.

Each day was a journey, she had endured,
For she had experienced a soul's connection
As she had now, drifted to a different level,
Where she no longer feared, being an option.

So,
You shall always be in my prayers, she said
As she rowed her boat away,
To ease him of his dilemma
To ease him of his dilemma.

35. THE GREAT INDIAN BANYAN TREE

Oh! The great Indian Banyan tree,
The blanket of green on Thee,
Each bud breaks into an era,
One by one, of the stories untold.

Memories splutter,
Behold! O' Gracious One,
For you are home to dreams, too many,
Treasures beneath lie deep,
For you are home to dreams, too many.

Oh! the great Indian Banyan tree,
You walk with poise and dignity,
Silently strengthening your roots,
As you churn the spiritual wheel
We all began to heal....

For it is then time for The Secret, to reveal
Let go, teaches us the banyan tree,
Let go, teaches us the banyan tree...!!!

36. OLYMPICS

I am the Olympics,
My daddy called me "Jeux Olympiques",
In Greece was I born,
In the 8th century B.C.

I adorn a flag as my armour,
Of Love & Unity,
With 5 circles, I embrace the world,
Different colour, different creed,
We play till we succeed.

To begin, a priestess then comes,
With her beauty, she lights up a lamp,
To illuminate the world as one,
Traditions in full galore.

CITIUS, ALTIUS, FORTIUS together we sing,
Faster we run,
Higher we jump,
&
Stronger we become!!

37. AWAAZ

Ik awaaz ho,
Meri dhadkanon ka saaz ho,
Mein aaj mein khud ko dhoondati,
Mere hone ka ehsaas ho.

Tum door ho ki paas ho,
Ho haqeeqat ya phir bus ek raaz ho,
Mein aaj mein khud ko dhoondati,
Mere hone ka ehsaas ho.

Ho prarthana meri, ya ho meri prerna
Jaanti hunt oh bus itna
Ki meri har sajri saver ki namaaz ho.

Ik awaaz ho
Meri dhadkanon ka saaz ho
Mein aaj mein khud ko dhoondati
Mere hone ka ehsaas ho

Tammana hai bus yehi
Rahun aagosh mein teri
Jab bhi is zindagi ki saanjh ho

Ek awaaz ho
Meri dhadkanon ka saaz ho.....

TRANSLATION POEM NO.37.

THE VOICE.

Are you a just a voice
Or the music to my soul
I look for myself in me today
My existence resonates from Thee.

Are you somewhere far away or are you very close
Are you for real or are you just a mystery
I look for myself in me today
My existence resonates from Thee.

Are you the prayers for me or are you the inspiration
All that I know is...
You are my each new day's Namaz(the prayer).

This heart desires to be,
Lying in your arms,
Whenever the night of my life dawns.

38. ZINDAGI

Zindagi ko jab guzarte dekha,
Awaaz lagayi paas bethaya,
Sawal tha bs yehi
Kahan thamogi?

Musqurqar boli...jo mein thak gayi,
Toh unn jazbaaton ka kya
Jo har morr pe umeed lagaye bethe hein!

Phir uthi aur chal parri,
Phir kisiko yeh sach samjhaane,
Phir kisi bhichr ko milane.

Raftaar se jo guzre zindagi,
Toh ganimat samjho,
Saanson ka yeh khel,
Phir dikha gayi yeh zindagi!

TRANSLATION POEM NO.38. LIFE

When I saw life going by,
Asked it to come and sit close to me.
One question that I asked,
"when will you ever pause"?

It smiled and said,"If I ever tire,
What happens to those who wait in faith"!

Then got up to leave,
And teach this truth to all,
To make two separated souls to meet again.

This game of speed,
Is a blessing,
The zest of life,
Taught once again!

39. KHARA BHYE JAGG MEIN

Khara bhai jagg mein har bandhan khara hoye,
Jo khoye meethas.
Sagar se bujhi na pyas kahu ki,
Sagar bhi khara hoye.

Jo pathar mein pa le khuda ko,
Va ki preet na sadharan hoye.
Pur na bujhe vo,
Jo har pal hi mazhab khoye.

Loot k fakir ko,
Kahe tu itraye?
Jholi mein bhar liye tune, navrang sahi,
Pur tere khoon mein na rang koi!

Tinke tinke vishwas se bane gharonde hoye,
Va kya samjhe lagan chakor ki,
Jo "mein" k nashe mein rahe khoye.

Maati kargaya wajood va mera
Maati pari roye,
Tu jo ronde aaj kisi ko,
Kal tu bhi toh maati mein hi soye.

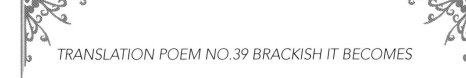

TRANSLATION POEM NO.39 BRACKISH IT BECOMES

Brackish becomes the relationships
Which looses its sweetness
The sea cannot quench its thirst
As briny is the sea.

The one who finds God in a rock
His love is not a mere emotion
But fails so understand such greatness
The one who looses faith every moment.

Why so much pride
In cheating a saint
In your bag of lies you filled colours of the rainbow
But in your veins flows a colourless liquid.

The nest is build with tiny twigs of faith
He fails to understand the dedication of the
Chakor(a bird that is in love with the moon)
Who is intoxicated in the love of self.

He crumbled my being to specks of dust
The mother earth wails,
"Today you bury someone's existence in me
Tomorrow the same fate awaits you!

40. SAWAL KAI

Lab pe hein sawal kai,
Kashish si hai jazbaaton mein,
Khoya khoya sa mann mera,
Umeed liye khwabon mein.

Lab pe hein sawal kai,
Kashish si hai jazbaaton mein.

Waqt bhi hai kuch yun guzra,
Kabhi apna sa kabhi paraya sa,
Kuch man ki kahi kuch keh na saki,
Kuch qismat ki thi saazish si,
Vo apna bhi ho na saka,
Na paraya usse keh hi sake.

Vo dil ki lagi na keh saka,
Hum dil ki lagi ka kya kahein,
Vo umeed meri, vo jazbaat mere,
Vo peer mera, vo paigambar bhi,
Jo sab hai mera,
Toh kya reh gaya, tera, mere rasooq!

Jo naam tera aaye labbon pe,
Toh musqan yeh meri,
Le aayi phir...
Lab pe sawal kai
Lab pe vo sawal kai!

Translation poem no.40

I HAVE QUESTIONS MANY

Questions I adorn on my lips today
Yearning in the feelings
Lost I am in thoughts
Hope in my dreams.

Questions I adorn on my lips today
The time that swept by
Sometimes felt own sometimes like a stranger
Could express some, some thoughts could never do.
The fortune too conspired
Could never make him mine
&
Neither could ever let go.

Never could he express the love
What do I do about being so lovelorn
He is my hope, my desire
My saint and my Lord is he.
When all belongs to me, O'My beloved
What is left of Thee I ask!

As your name brushes past these lips
The escaping smile then brings
Questions too many
The lips then hold questions too many!

41. QASID

Yeh andaaz -e-ulfat bhi kya khoob rahi Galib,
Bikhri umeedon k saath, rahguzar chalta hi gaya,
Jab aankh khuli, zindagi dehleez k uss paar mili.

Shab -e -hayat mein bhi rahi raunaq
Mere masood, tere hi noor se,
Alphaaz - e -gumm peerote rahe,
Dubokar raat ki gehri sihayi mein,
Kahin yeh ashqon ka abrr,
Pheeka na karde, haal -e -byan.

Bus itna qarm karde maula,
Saanson ka jab yeh qafan choote,
Ik moothi mitti hi bhej dein vo
Qasid k haath,
Meri qabr sajane ko
Bus ik muthi mitti....!!!

TRANSLATION: THE MESSANGER

Oh what an expression of love Galib!
With lost hope walked I, on the lonely path of life,
When I woke up,
Life was on the other side of time.

Translation contd. Poem 41.

The dark nights were lit up by my beloved's charm.
Where IKept beading my words of pain,
In the dark ink of the nights,
May the cloud of tears that I hold within,
Not dilute the painful expression.

Just do me a favour Lord!
The day the soul leaves the dying corpse,
May he send, just a handful of soil,
Through the messenger,
To adorn my grave.
Just one handful ofsoil.

42. SACH

Gumshuda sa hai sach,
Jhoot ki is mehfil mein,
Sehma sa, darra hua sa,
Apni awaaz ko talaashta huwa, yeh sach.

Shor hai yeh kesa,
Hahakaar macha hua,
Be imaan hua har shaye,
Hai yeh kesi saazish mein, phasa hua sa ik sach.

Larkharate qadmon se vo chalta hi raha,
Na khoya aapa apna,
Khokar bhi apno ka saath.

Waqt ne phir li karwat,
Mehfil ki shamma, suraj ko kab taq thi rok paati
Har mukhauta pighalne laga tha
Jhoot gira phir muh k bal,
Hua jo sach ka saamna.

Sach ne ki phir awaaz buland,
Haar kar bhi jo haar na mane,
Hoti sach ki pehchaan yehi,
Hoti sach ki pehchaaan yehi....!!

Translation: Poem No.42.

THE TRUTH

Lost is the truth
In the gathering of lies,
Scared and timid
Looking around for the sound of its voice.

Why this chaos, so much noise around
Dishonest is every point
Oh what is this conspiracy against the truth!

It stumbled but walked its path still
Never lost its sanity
Having lost those very own.

Then the tables turned,
How long could the light of the gathering
stop the Sun from raising again
Every mask then began to melt,
The lie fell flat on the ground, coming face to face to The Truth.

The truth then roared!
The one who never accepts defeat having lost a few,
That is the Identity of Truth,
That is the identity of Truth.

43. BADAL

Badalon ka haal na pooch, mere dost
Abrr ne bara honsla hai kiya,
Ab k jo barsa, toh samjhlejo
Koi daaman hai phir choota! (22 words)

Translation: *THE CLOUDS*

Oh please don't ask the clouds how they have been
In endurance have they lived
The showers today are tear
Somewhere again someone has lost a beloved!

Printed in the United States
By Bookmasters